Well Made, Fair Trade

My T-SHIRT and other clothes

W
FRANKLIN WATTS
LONDON • SYDNEY

First published in 2015 by
Franklin Watts
338 Euston Road
London
NW1 3BH

Franklin Watts Australia
Level 17/207 Kent Street
Sydney
NSW 2000

HB ISBN 978 1 4451 3273 0
Library ebook ISBN 978 1 4451 3275 4

A CIP catalogue record for this book is
available from the British Library.

Series Editor: Julia Bird
Packaged by: Q2A Media

Picture credits: Front Cover: Elena Rostunova, Pressmaster, S1001, Africa Studio, Milosz_G/Shutterstock.
Back Cover: Photobank.ch/Shutterstock. Title Page: Alhovik, Karkas, Robert_s, Loukia, Bohbeh/Shutterstock.
Imprint Page: Africa Studio/Shutterstock. P4(R): Artjazz/Shutterstock, P4(TL): Mike Flippo/Shutterstock, P4(BL):
Mike Flippo/Shutterstock, P4(CL): Urfin/Shutterstock; P5(TL): Fairtrade Organic, P5(B): Ekler/Shutterstock, P5(CR):
Urfin/Shutterstock, P5(TR): Mike Flippo/Shutterstock, P5(C): Flas100/Shutterstock; P6 Mandy Godbehear/
Shutterstock; P7: Lizette Potgieter/Shutterstock; P8(B): 2001–2014 People Tree and others, P8(T) Fairtrade Organic,
P8(BKGRD): Surrphoto/Shutterstock; P9(TL): TongChuwit/Shutterstock, P9(C): Rapanui Clothing,
P9(B): Rapanui Clothing, P9(TR): Q2a Media; P10–11(BKGRD): Flas100/Shutterstock, P10(C): 2014 LS&CO,
P10(B): Nikonova Margarita/Shutterstock; P11(L): Africa Studio/Shutterstock, P11(R): Halina Yakushevich/
Shutterstock; P12(T):WarOnWant.org, P12(BR): Kevin Rijnders/Kuyichi; P12–13(BKGRD): My Life Graphic/
shutterstock, P13(B): Andrew Biraj/Reuters; P14(L): Aleksandra Zaitseva/Shutterstock, P14(R): Amorfati.art/
Shutterstock; P15(T): Foto76/Shutterstock, P15(B): Sigit Pamungkas/Reuters; P14–15(BKGRD): Antonio Villani/
Fotolia; P16–17(BKGRD): Antonio Villani/Fotolia, P16(T): Havaianas, P16(C): Havaianas, P16(B): Ocean Sole LTD;
P17: Dr Martin Kunz; P18–19(BKGRD): Shooarts/Shutterstock; P18(B): EvaKaufman/istock; P19(TR):
Huang Zheng/Shutterstock, P19(B): Ambika Canroy; P20(T): Kobby Dagan/Shutterstock, P20(BL): 2014 Turtle
Doves Ltd, P20(BR): TongChuwit/Shutterstock; P21(R): 2014 Peruvian Connection; P20–21(BKGRD): Shooarts/
Shutterstock, P21(BR): Joel Shawn/Shutterstock; P22(C): AMA/Shutterstock, P22(BKGRD): HomeArt/Shutterstock;
P23(T): Michael S. Yamashita/Corbis, P23(CT): TongChuwit/Shutterstock, P23(B): Dr. Morley Read/Shutterstock;
P24–25(BKGRD): HomeArt/Shutterstock, P24(T): Pete Niesen/Shutterstock; P25(T): Suvra Kanti Das/Zuma Press/
Corbis, P25(B): Studio Veja; P26: Fuyu Liu/Shutterstock, P26–27(BKGRD): Madlen/Shutterstock, P27(T): Dmitry
Naumov/Shutterstock, P27(B): Elena Mirage/Shutterstock; P28(T): Robert Harding Picture Library Ltd/Alamy,
P28(B): Jackiso/Shutterstock; P29(BL) TongChuwit/Shutterstock, P29(T): Papilio/Alamy, P29(C): Teresa Levite/
Shutterstock, P29(BR): Nomads Clothing; P30–31: Malgorzata Kistryn/Shutterstock; P32: Malgorzata Kistryn/
Shutterstock. Illustrations: all-free-downloads.com (P6–7(BKGRD), 9(BKGRD), 26–27(BKGRD), 28–29(BKGRD)).

Printed in Malaysia

Franklin Watts is a division of Hachette Children's Books, an Hachette UK company.www.hachette.co.uk

Contents

Words in **bold** can be found in the glossary on page 30.

Why buy fair trade?

Many people work to put our clothes and shoes together before they reach the shops. Fair trade organisations, such as the Fairtrade Foundation, aim to make sure that everyone involved, from the farmer to the garment worker, is well treated.

Fair trade organisations work to encourage clothing companies to produce clothes that are kind to the environment and to the people who make them.

What is fair trade?

Most of the clothes we buy are produced in **developing countries**, such as India and China. Often the people who work in fields and factories where the materials for our clothes are sourced and put together are paid very little and have poor working conditions. Fair trade aims to make sure workers are paid a fair price for the work they do and that their working conditions are clean and safe.

Labelling fashion

So far, not many fashion items come with a fair trade label, but look out for the FAIRTRADE Mark, World Fair Trade Organisation or Fair Wear Foundation logos and marks in clothes shops or on items of clothing. These labels all show that a product has been produced according to different fair trade standards.

Look out for fair trade marks and labels, such as this FAIRTRADE Mark, on clothes and footwear when you go shopping.

Fair trade schemes

This book describes some of the problems faced by people in the developing world, who make or provide the **raw materials** for many of our clothes. It explains some fair trade solutions and will help you to understand why fair trade is so important, and how you can help by being careful about where you shop and what you buy.

This map shows the countries mentioned in this book that are involved in fair trade clothing projects.

Cotton T-shirt

The T-shirt has been around for over 100 years. It started out as a tight-fitting undershirt, worn by American sailors and soldiers.

Most T-shirts are made from cotton and dyed many different colours. T-shirts are named after the T-shape made by the body and sleeves.

How is your T-shirt made?

The cotton plant takes about 200 days to grow. Its 'boll' or seed splits open and **fibres** burst out that look like cotton wool balls. This cotton is **harvested** by hand or machine. Seeds inside the cotton are separated and used to make cottonseed oil, while the raw cotton fibre is sent to a textile mill. Here, it will be pulled, stretched and twisted into yarn, then dyed to make the cotton fabric for a T-shirt. The fabric is sewn into a garment in a factory, often in India or China.

Where does cotton come from?

Cotton grows in warm climates all around the world. Countries such as China, India, the USA and Uzbekistan, in central Asia, are the largest producers. In many developing countries, such as India and parts of Africa and South America, cotton is still picked by hand, mainly by women and children. The pickers are often badly paid and many live in **poverty**.

Chemical dangers

Cotton plants are often treated with large quantities of **pesticides** to prevent them from being damaged by insects and diseases. However, chemicals in the pesticides can cause headaches, sickness and breathing difficulties for the workers who apply them.

Pesticides that have been banned in some countries because they are dangerous to human and animal health may still be shipped to developing countries where they are sold for use in the cotton fields. Workers who spray the pesticides often have no training or protective equipment. Pesticides wash off the fields into local rivers and water supplies and can have devastating environmental effects.

Environment matters

Non-organic cotton farming uses nearly a quarter of all the world's **insecticides** and about 10 per cent of the world's pesticides. Pesticide Action Network UK (PAN UK) and the Soil Association encourage farmers to use **non-toxic** pesticides. This is not only better for the environment, wildlife and the health of farm workers, it also reduces debt as toxic pesticides are very expensive to buy and farmers use a huge amount on their crops.

In many countries picking cotton is done by women and children. These children are picking cotton in Uzbekistan.

Case study: Agrocel, India

FAIRTRADE
Certified Cotton

The Ranchhod family lives on a small cotton farm in Gujarat in western India. Growing cotton is hard, especially at harvest time, when work starts at 6am and there's hardly a break until 4pm. Khima Ranchhod sells his cotton through Fairtrade to Agrocel, a **co-operative** that encourages local workers to produce **organic**, Fairtrade cotton. Khima and his family earn a better price for their crop now, because the co-operative sells the cotton to wealthier buyers in the developed world. Today, Khima's cotton can be found in products made for companies such as People Tree and Marks & Spencer.

Low costs, high profits

Agrocel has helped Khima to become an organic grower and shown him how to keep his production costs low. With higher profits, Khima can now afford to buy organic manure to help the cotton grow. Water is scarce, but organic manure helps keep moisture in the soil. Khima, and his wife Jamnaben, hope they will soon have enough money to send their daughters to school, and perhaps put a tiled roof on their house.

Organic farming means that fewer pesticides and chemicals are sprayed on the cotton plants. This means workers who pick the cotton by hand are less likely to bcome ill.

Re-use, recycle

What can you do with a tired old T-shirt? You can put it in a clothes bank, give it to a charity shop – or you can cut off the sleeves, deepen the neck and sew up the bottom of the T-shirt to make a colourful bag!

Good buy!

Rapanui calls itself an 'eco-fashion company'. It was set up in 2008 by brothers Rob and Mart Drake-Knight. All Rapanui T-shirts are made in India, using handpicked organic cotton that is transported by camel and cart to a factory powered by wind energy. The company uses fair trade and Fair Wear suppliers, so they know that the people who provide their cotton have been paid fairly and that the cotton production has not damaged the environment.

This T-shirt is a tribute to the work done by Sea Shepherd, a group that protects whales.

Rapanui designed this T-shirt to support the Marine Conservation Society (MCS). They give 50 per cent of all profits made on these T-shirts to the MCS.

Denim jeans

Around the world, the market for denim jeans is projected to reach US $56 billion by 2018. Around 17 per cent of all cotton produced is made into denim.

The first jeans

The first jeans were made from a thick, heavy material used for tents and wagon covers during the **gold rush** in California in the 1850s. They were intended as strong, hardwearing work clothes for farmers, miners and cowboys. The denim company, Levi Strauss, produced the first jeans with **rivets** in 1873. They were designed to be even stronger and less likely to rip. They were produced in blue denim, canvas and brown duck (a heavy cotton material).

The world's oldest surviving pair of Levi's jeans. They date back to 1879 and are called 'buckle-backs'. These jeans have been valued at around £88,500.

Rivets are permanent metal fasteners used to strengthen jeans. They are usually found at the corners and sides of the pockets to hold the fabric together where it is too thick to be sewn.

Where do your jeans come from?

Today, cotton could be picked in the USA, then flown to India to be made up into fabric, with thread coming from Turkey or Hungary, dyes from Spain and a zip from Japan (the brass coming from zinc and copper mined in Australia or Namibia). Finally, buttons from China or Africa might be added.

How are jeans made?

Denim fabric is woven from two cotton yarns. One is dyed indigo blue, which shows on the outside, and the other is white, which shows on the inside. The fabric is cut into shaped pieces, which are put together by hand, then sewn together on special sewing machines. Zips, pockets and rivets are added, and seams and hems stitched up. Then the jeans are washed to fade the denim and tagged ready for shipping.

A survey found that, on average, people in the USA have seven pairs of jeans in their wardrobe.

Working conditions

Some jeans are **sandblasted** to make them look worn and faded. Over many years dust from the sand can get into workers' lungs, causing a deadly disease called silicosis. Sufferers cough and have trouble breathing. Factories rarely provide health care or protective clothing. In 2012, the Clean Clothes Campaign called on manufacturers to stop sandblasting by changing the designs of their jeans. They **petitioned** fashion companies to ban sandblasting on their garments altogether, and to ask local workers' organisations to make sure factories followed this ban. Many jean companies, including Benetton, Gucci, H&M and Levi-Strauss & Co have agreed.

Many jeans are made in over-crowded factories in countries such as Bangladesh, Turkey and China, where pay is low and shifts can last for up to 12 hours a day.

Good buy!

A company called Kuyichi was set up in 2001 after its Dutch founders could not persuade large fashion manufacturers to switch to organic cotton. The company makes jeans using organic cotton and natural dyes that do not risk workers' health. Water in their factories is cleaned and recycled. Kuyichi is a member of the Fair Wear Foundation.

Kiyuchi make jeans from recycled denim as well as organic cotton.

Case study: Rana Plaza, Dhaka, Bangladesh

Nasima Begum worked in the Rana Plaza factory sewing up jeans. One day, after a crack appeared in the walls of the factory building, her bosses sent her home. She was terrified, but returned to work next day on her bosses' orders. The whole family relied on her earnings of $110 a month and she was scared of losing her job. Sadly, the building collapsed and Nasima's body was never found.

Nasima's devastated family has not been able to claim any **compensation**. Some international retailers have paid compensation to the workers and their families, but this is not compulsory, as they are not held responsible for the accident.

Back to school

Verité-Sheva is a Bangladeshi programme that aims to encourage children affected by the building collapse to stay in school. Many were choosing to work to earn money to support their families, but by providing two good meals a day in the school, many children are now going back to study. The programme is also working to encourage safety in the workplace, and is teaching managers in some of the largest clothing companies about health and safety. The programme is supported by some international retailers, such as Primark.

Over 2,200 workers were pulled alive from the wreckage of Rana Plaza, but over 1,000 died. Many survivors will have a disability for the rest of their lives.

Flip-flops

Flip-flops are cheap to mass-produce and are worn by millions of people around the world. In many hot developing countries flip-flops might be the only shoes that people own.

What are flip-flops made of?

Flip-flops can be made from many different materials, but most have plastic, natural or **synthetic rubber** soles. Synthetic rubber is produced from petroleum, but natural rubber comes from trees grown in **plantations** in countries such as Thailand, Vietnam, Sri Lanka, Liberia and Guatemala.

Flip-flops take their design from a traditional Japanese sandal with a sole made of wood or straw, and a fabric thong.

How is rubber produced?

Each morning, in a rubber plantation, the trees are cut so that the sap, or latex, trickles out into a cup fixed to the tree. This is called tapping. Workers collect the latex, mix it with acid and roll it through a machine to form a sheet.

Plantation workers in developing countries in Africa and South-east Asia often live in shacks supplied by the plantation owners, without running water or electricity.

Latex is a white liquid that is tapped from trees and used to make rubber.

Case study: Harbel, Liberia, Africa

In Liberia, workers on rubber plantations worked 12-hour shifts for low wages, and were sometimes ordered to double production for no extra pay. Each worker was expected to tap up to 800 trees in a shift, and carry buckets weighing 30kg each for over two kilometres to the weighing station. Sometimes workers brought their children to help, because their employer's demands were too high.

Union agreement

In 2010, an agreement was signed between the Firestone Natural Rubber Company in Harbel and the employees' union. The agreement banned children from working on the plantations, reduced the amount of latex employees were expected to collect and provided better systems of transport.

Before the agreement workers carried heavy buckets of latex to be weighed. Today, tractors and lorries carry the rubber to the weighing station.

Fair trade flip-flops

The Havaianas factory in Brazil started making flip-flops in 1962 and is now the largest manufacturer of flip-flops in the world, making an average of six pairs a second. The Havaianas factory follows many fair trade practices and donates money to the Institute for Ecological Studies which helps to protect the environment in Brazil. The company has also given money to build sports facilities to help keep children and young people off the streets.

Havaianas in Brazil produces 184 million pairs of flip-flops a year.

Good buy!

Thousands of old flip-flops wash up on the beaches of Kenya, East Africa, every year, ruining the beach and harming coastal wildlife. After some local people began using the flip-flops to make children's toys, they eventually formed a company called Ocean Sole. Now they sell recycled flip-flop products around the world.

Environment matters

In Kerala, south-western India, a company called Guru makes traditional Indian-designed flip-flops. They use natural rubber from their own farms and plant a tree for every pair of flip-flops sold. If you throw away old Guru flip-flops, they break down naturally.

Case study: Frocester Rubber Plantation, Sri Lanka

Madhura is 10 years old and she has lived all her life on the rubber plantation where her parents work. Madhura's family are Tamil, which means that they do not have the same rights as other Sri Lankan people. The state even refused to supply them with electricity. Luckily, Frocester is a fair trade plantation.

Fair trade is helping Madhura to get a better education, which might mean she can earn enough to help support her family when she is older.

Electricity supplies

The workers here receive a premium from the rubber they produce, which is given back to the workers' community. In 2011, money earned from fair trade enabled the plantation workers to have their own electricity supply installed. Now Madhura can do her homework and iron her school uniform after dark.

Fluffy jumper

We all know that wool comes from sheep, but did you know that your fluffiest jumper could be made from rabbit fur or wool from an alpaca?

Where does angora come from?

Angora rabbits originally come from Turkey. Today, Chinese farms and factories keep around 50 million angora rabbits, providing 90 per cent of the world's yearly production of 2,500-3,000 tonnes of angora wool. Some of the wool is **exported** for processing in Europe and Japan. Angora rabbits are also farmed in Argentina, Chile, the Czech Republic and Hungary.

Angora wool comes from rabbits, while angora goats produce mohair. Wool from angora rabbits is 800 per cent warmer than wool from sheep.

How is angora produced?

Angora rabbits need regular grooming to stop their fur from matting. They **moult** naturally every three months and at this stage their fur can be gently plucked by hand or sheared. Recent reports have shown that rabbits in some factories live in terrible conditions. The animals are kept in tiny, dirty cages that are rarely cleaned out. The wire on the bottom of the cage can cut their feet, and they are given no space to run and play. To speed up collection, the rabbits' fur is collected in a way that hurts the rabbits and leaves them shocked and in pain. A healthy angora rabbit can live up to ten years, but most farmed rabbits die within two years.

In 2013, the animal rights organisation PETA (People for the **Ethical** Treatment of Animals) exposed these conditions, and high-street stores such as H&M, Esprit and New Look stopped selling angora products. Twelve clothing companies have now banned angora products from their range completely.

Angora rabbits have different-coloured fur, from white, tan and grey to brown to black. Many garments made from their wool use these natural colours but for some garments the wool is dyed different colours.

Good buy!

Ambika Conroy keeps her own rabbits on her farm in New York State, USA. She gently shears the rabbits' fur every three months, then spins and knits it into hats, scarves, jumpers, jackets and legwarmers to sell via her website.

Some of Ambika Conroy's products made from the wool from her angora rabbits.

Alpaca farmers in Peru

We also get wool for fluffy jumpers from alpacas. Alpaca farmers in the Peruvian Andes are poor and there is little education available because they live in such a remote area. Today, help for the herders comes from a private enterprise called Pacomarca that provides training in the latest techniques of shearing, feeding and looking after alpacas. It also helps to train farmers in house-building and supports local schools and teaching. In addition, a group called Inca Tops has donated wool and set up textile workshops for mothers in small mountain villages to teach them how to knit jumpers.

Alpacas have been bred in South America for thousands of years. Although it is similar to sheep's wool, alpaca wool is warmer, naturally water-repellant and more fire resistant.

Good buy!

Turtle Doves, based in Shropshire, UK, make accessories, such as fingerless gloves and scarves out of old jumpers. Turtle Dove products are sold mainly online.

Re-use, recycle

It's easy to recycle an old woollen jumper by unpicking the yarn and re-using it. You can even buy recycled wool on eBay that has been unravelled for you. Then you can knit up your own woolly items, such as a scarf or mittens.

Case study: Peruvian Connection, USA

This alpaca cardigan comes from a US company called Peruvian Connection. Company founders, Biddy and Anne Hurlbut, have been importing alpaca products from Peru since 1976. The company's jumpers and cardigans are made by Peruvian workers who are paid a good price for their work, given bonuses, hot meals and help with transport and childcare.

Local projects

Peruvian Connection supports many local projects, including an orphanage and a programme for teaching disabled children. It also supports Pro Mujer Peru, an organisation which enables women to operate small businesses by helping them find loans, business training and affordable healthcare.

Dyed alpaca yarn. Alpaca wool is softer and warmer than sheep's wool.

Peruvian Connection garments are all made by skilled Peruvian workers.

Trainers

Around 350 million sports shoes are sold every year in the US alone. You don't have to play a sport to wear trainers, but once your trainers have worn out, recycle them – they could be turned into a new sports track!

Today, many sports have their own specially designed trainers.

Fair trade for feet

When it comes to fair trade, there is a long way to go in the footwear industry, from getting a good deal for employees assembling trainers in factories to protecting the rights of animals who are treated brutally in order to provide cheap leather. Independent companies are making a difference but there is still a long way to go to improve conditions for everyone involved in the **supply chain.** Many people still work long hours in unsafe conditions and are poorly paid.

Where do trainers come from?

Large, well-known footwear companies often use factories in China, India, Cambodia, Vietnam, the Philippines and Indonesia to make their shoes. Manufacturers like to produce trainers in these countries because factory production is cheap – employers are often not required by law to look after the workers, so production costs are low.

How are trainers made?

Making trainers is a complicated business, and producing the sole is particularly difficult. It could have three layers: an insole; a midsole with a core of gel, foam, liquid **silicone** or even compressed air; and an outsole made of rubber.

The upper, or top part, of the trainers might be canvas, synthetic fabric or leather, cut to shape with holes punched for the laces, then stitched together. The heel and toe are stiffened before the upper is heated and moulded into shape. The sole is attached to the upper, and laces are added by hand.

Workers in China check finished trainers as they roll past on a conveyor belt.

In some countries, valuable rainforest is burnt and cleared so that it can be used as grazing land for cattle. Their skins are used to create the leather used in making trainers and other shoes.

Re-use, recycle

VivoBarefoot shoes make the nylon that covers their trainers from recycled plastic bottles. The soles are made from natural latex and rice husks, and the insoles are non-toxic, **biodegradable** gel pads. Even the shoetree that holds the shape of the shoe is made from recycled cardboard.

Processing leather

Leather is animal skin that has been through a process called 'tanning'. Tanning makes the animal skin clean and strong so it can be made into clothes, shoes and bags. However, unprotected workers can suffer from the chemicals that are used in the tanning process. One substance, **chromium**, has been linked to cancer, asthma, bronchitis and pneumonia. It is a particular problem for workers in some Indian, Pakistani and South American tanning factories. In addition, dangerous chemical waste has been found flowing out of the factories. Chromium in the waste can **contaminate** nearby soil, and food that grows in the soil. It can also pollute local drinking water, endangering the people and animals that drink it, as well as the fish that live in it.

Environment matters

The Blacksmith Institute is an international non-government organisation (NGO) that aims to find solutions to the problems of toxic waste. Their researchers have found ways of cleaning up toxic chromium by treating it either with another type of chromium or with charcoal from burned animal bones. Since treating **groundwater** from 300 tanneries around Kanpur, in India, some wells were tested and showed hardly any trace of chromium at all.

Case study: Tanning factories in Hazaribagh, Bangladesh

Leather factories are booming in Bangladesh because labour is cheap. Around 15,000 people work in the 150 tanning factories of Hazaribagh. They work without eye protection or facemasks, using dangerous chemicals such as chromium.

Burning skin

At one tannery, 17-year-old Jahad says acid in the water makes his skin burn. He suffers from asthma and has rashes on his body, but he has to work at the factory because there are no other jobs available.

Now the factory has plans to move to new premises, where working conditions will be much better. This is as a result of the Rana Plaza disaster (see page 13), which has put pressure on international manufacturers to improve working conditions in Bangladesh.

These workers are soaking animal skins in baths of water mixed with chemicals. They wear very little protective clothing.

Good buy!

Veja's fair trade trainers cost three to four times more to produce than ordinary trainers, but the company saves money by not advertising. The shoes sell by word of mouth.

A French company, Veja, make their trainers in Brazil. The canvas uppers are made from organic fair trade cotton, and fair trade rubber is used for the soles. Fair trade leather is harder to source. Veja are careful where their leather comes from, and are working to improve their supply chain.

Silk

It may be hard to believe, but lovely soft silk is made from the cocoons of caterpillars. Thousands of cocoons are needed to make one simple dress.

It takes about 3,000 silkworm cocoons to make 500 grams of silk. It has been calculated that it would take 5,000 cocoons to make one silk dressing gown.

Where is silk produced?

A Chinese legend tells how silk was discovered in 2640 BCE, when a silkworm cocoon fell into Empress Si Ling Chi's hot cup of tea and started to unravel. The empress twisted the fibres together and wove it into fabric.

Today, silk is produced in over 60 countries around the world. Most silk still comes from China, which produces three times more silk than India, the next biggest producer. Silk comes from other countries, too, such as Thailand, Uzbekistan, Brazil and Vietnam.

How is silk made?

Bombyx mori silkworms are a type of caterpillar. After the caterpillars hatch, they eat lots of mulberry leaves and grow to ten thousand times their birth size in about 30-40 days. Then the silkworm takes three days to build a cocoon while it turns into a moth. The cocoon is then boiled and the silk thread is unravelled. One cocoon will provide a strand of thread around 500 metres long. The strands are dyed and woven by hand or machine to make silk fabric.

Millions of silkworm cocoons are left to grow in silkworm farms.

Problems with production

Workers in silk mills can develop lung infections, caused by fine dust that comes from the fabric. The longer a worker stays in the same job, the higher the chances they will become ill. In Mumbai, India, one survey found that 30 per cent of workers in spinning, winding and **carding** departments had breathing difficulties.

Dyes and chemicals used to colour the fabric can also cause rashes and sickness. Possible solutions to these problems include keeping dust levels low and giving workers protective clothing to wear. At the moment there are no fair trade schemes set up to help workers in bigger factories, but some smaller, independent companies are finding better ways to work.

The effects of the dust in silk mills can be reduced if workers wear facemasks and move around the mill doing different jobs.

Case study: Sawang Boran, Thailand

Sawang Boran in Thai means 'ancient brilliance' and the project, which was set up in 2008, encourages young women to learn traditional silk weaving techniques that will help them to earn a living. Yaa Lai, who is 87, and other local weavers are teaching valuable skills to younger workers. By selling their fabrics and silk products around the world, the women are turning silk-making into a business. Profits from the sale of their silk products are put back into the project.

This young girl is making silk in the traditional way on a loom.

Fair trade, fair price

Through the Sawang Boran project, women are trained and given interest-free loans to start their businesses and buy equipment, such as looms and sewing machines.

The project holds regular meetings where the women can share skills and discuss ideas and problems, as well as calculate their earnings. They are paid a fair price for their silk and work a maximum of 5–6 hours a day, leaving time for them to spend with their children and families.

Before the project began, the women used synthetic dyes and chemical bleaches. Now their dyes and silk are all organic.

Good buy!

Silk made by the Masuta **collective** in India comes from tussah silkworms that live wild in the forest. These silkworms transform into moths and leave the cocoon before the silk is collected. The collective was set up to help poor women find work. By 2010, 2,500 women were producing tussah silk. The women had training in how to rear silkworms; trees were planted to feed the caterpillars and netting put up to protect them.

Tussah silkworms eat oak leaves. A substance called tannin in the leaves makes the silk naturally honey-coloured. Tussah silk yarn is thicker than mulberry silk. It can be dyed and made into fabric for clothes.

Re-use, recycle

In India, at the time of the August full moon, girls traditionally throw out their old saris and their brothers give them a new one. Nomads Clothing now has a range of clothes made from these recycled silk saris. This company has been producing fair trade clothes for 20 years, to help people from poorer communities support themselves.

Silk is lightweight but hardwearing. It is warm in winter and cool in summer.

Glossary

biodegradable A material that can be broken down naturally by living things

carding Brushing or combing yarn to make it smooth before spinning

chromium A shiny metallic element

collective A group of usually small, local companies that work together

compensation Money given to workers by a company or government to help them cope with the results of an accident at work

contaminate To pollute with a poisonous substance

co-operative A group of people, or organisations, working together and sharing any benefits or profits evenly between them.

developing countries Parts of the world where most people are not well off, but where local resources are being used to build up different industries

ethical Thinking about what is the right thing to do, such as paying workers a fair wage even though this means less profit

export Produce that is sent out of a country to be sold in other parts of the world

fibres Fine threads which make up a yarn or fabric.

gold rush When gold was discovered in California, USA, in 1848. Thousands of people rushed to California to search for gold in the hope of getting rich quick.

groundwater Water that collects under the ground and in cracks in the soil or rocks

harvested When crops are collected

insecticides Sprays that stop insects and bugs eating and damaging crops

mass produce To make a lot of one product quickly and usually cheaply in a factory

moult To shed fur ready for new fur to grow

non-organic Crops sprayed with insecticides and pesticides that could damage the local environment and wildlife

non-toxic Something that will not damage the environment, harm wildlife or make people ill

organic Crops which are produced without using chemicals

pesticides Chemicals used to stop insects and diseases damaging crops

petition To send out a petition – a request for change signed by lots of people that is sent to a large organisation or government

plantation Huge area of the same sort of trees grown for a single crop

poverty The state of being poor

premium An extra payment on top of the normal price for goods

raw materials The basic (unprocessed) materials that are used to make a product

rivet A small metal plate used to hold traditional jeans together

sandblast Apply a jet of sand powered by air or steam to roughen or clean

silicone A tough, artificial substance

supply chain The journey of an object from the sourcing of materials to when it reaches the shops

synthetic rubber Material that appears to be like rubber, but is made through a chemical process

tannery A place where animal skins and hides are processed and turned into leather

Websites

To learn more about the work of the Fairtrade Foundation look here: **www.fairtrade.org.uk**

For how to turn your T-shirt into a shopping bag look here: **www.instructables.com/id/FASTEST-RECYCLED-T-SHIRT-TOTE-BAG**

Find out more about Rapanui, how they started, the organisations they support and the clothes they make here: **www.rapanuiclothing.com/about.html**

Find out more about Ocean Sole flip-flop products here: **www.ocean-sole.com**

Read about the Clean Clothes Campaign here: **www.cleanclothes.org**

To find out more about Kuyichi Jeans, including how to buy them, look here: **www.kuyichi.com/dashboard**

To find out more about the Fair Wear Foundation and the companies that are members, check here: **www.fairwear.org**

See angora collected in an animal-friendly way: **http://thekidshouldseethis.com/post/69074981856**

Find things to do with your old jumpers here: **http://www.youtube.com/watch?v=WyZKq63447w**

Find out more about the policy behind Nomads Clothing: **http://www.nomadsclothing.com/fair-trade-policy**

Learn more about the organisations that the Havianas company helps here: **http://en-gb.havaianas.com/en-GB/responsibility/**

See silkworms at work here: **www.sciencechannel.com/tv-shows/how-do-they-do-it/videos/how-do-they-do-it-silk-from-worm-spit.htm**

Every effort has been made by the Publishers to ensure that the websites are suitable for children, and that they contain no inappropriate or offensive material. However, because of the nature of the Internet, it is impossible to guarantee that the contents of these sites will not be altered. We strongly advise that Internet access is supervised by a responsible adult.

Index